INVASION!

The Vikings

KAREN BRYANT-MOLE

Wayland

Invasion!

The Saxons
The Vikings
The Normans
The Romans

Cover design: Simon Balley
Book design: Malcolm Walker
Editor: Deb Elliott

Text is based on *The Vikings* in the Invaders and Settlers series published in 1992.

Picture acknowledgements
Aerofilms 6; Ancient Art and Architecture Collection 4 (bottom), 12, 14; C M Dixon title page, 5 (top), 10 (both), 20-21, 30, 31; Calderdale Leisure Services 29; Michael Holford 13 (left), 28; Werner Forman Archive contents page (top and bottom), 4 (top), 5 (bottom), 8 (both), 11 (both), 13 (right); York Archaeological Trust contents page (middle), 9, 15, 16, 19, 20 (left), 21 (both), 22 (both), 23, 25. The artwork on pages 6, 7, 9, 14, 17-18 is by Peter Bull, and pages 24, 26-7 is by Peter Dennis.

First published in 1995 by
Wayland (Publishers) Limited,
61 Western Road, Hove, East Sussex, BN3 1JD

© Copyright Wayland (Publishers) Limited

British Library Cataloguing in Publication Data
  Bryant-Mole, Karen
  Viking Invaders. – (Invasion! Series)
  I. Title II. Series
  941.01

ISBN 0 7502 1471 6

Typeset by Kudos Editorial Services
Printed in Italy

Opposite:
Top: A Viking carving of a ship.
Middle: A page from the Lindisfarne
          Gospels.
Bottom: A soapstone bowl.

Contents

THE VIKINGS ARRIVE........................4

THE VIKINGS' HOMELAND 7

VIKING GODS 10

VIKING WEAPONS 12

VIKING TOWNS 15

VIKING CRAFTS 20

WORKING OUT DATES 22

HOME LIFE 25

THE END OF THE STORY 28

GLOSSARY 30

BOOKS TO READ 30

PLACES TO VISIT 31

INDEX 32

The Vikings arrive

The word Viking means 'pirate'. The Vikings were fierce raiders who crossed the sea from their homelands in Sweden, Norway and Denmark to invade the coasts of England, Scotland, Wales and Ireland.

One of the places they invaded was the island of Lindisfarne, which is off the north-east coast of England. Many religious men, called monks, lived on Lindisfarne.

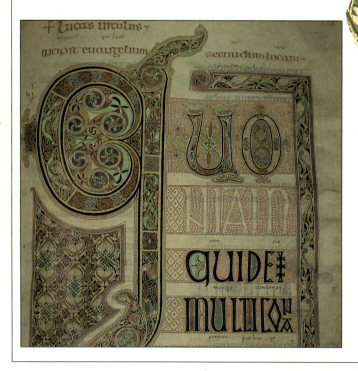

◄ This page from the Lindisfarne Gospels was drawn by monks.

The Vikings travelled in longships. The main photograph below shows the remains of a Viking ship. The carving on the left shows a Viking ship in full sail. Viking ships could also be rowed using oars.

▼ The carving on this tombstone shows Viking warriors.

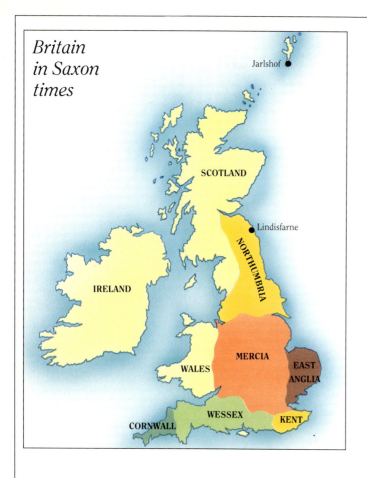

Britain in Saxon times

From their bases in Scotland the Vikings began making raids on England. Eventually they settled in England, too.

At the time of the first Viking invasions, people known as Saxons lived in most of England and southern Scotland. The people of northern Scotland were called Picts.

At first, the Vikings were raiders who returned to their own homelands with the money and treasures they had stolen. Then they began to stay and set up new homes. They first settled in the Scottish islands of the Orkneys and the Shetlands.

▲ A Viking site in the Shetlands.

The Vikings' homeland

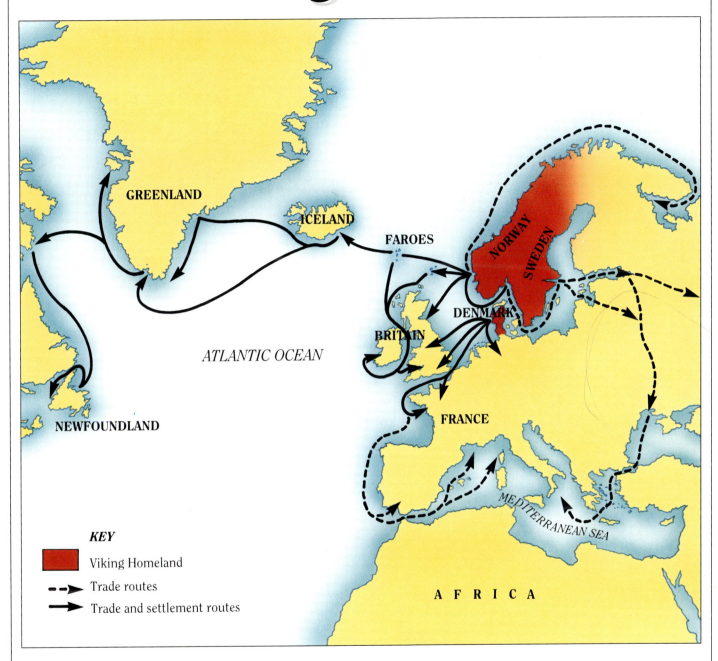

The Vikings came from the northern countries of Norway, Sweden and Denmark. As well as sailing to Britain, they sailed to Iceland and Greenland. They probably also reached a part of Canada which is now called Newfoundland.

Not all Vikings were raiders. Some stayed in their homelands and farmed the land. Others became merchants. They travelled long distances to sell goods such as furs and objects made from wood, metal or stone.

▼ A soapstone bowl

▲ These scales were used by a Viking merchant.

Hnefetafl

Hnefetafl was a Viking board game. There were white pieces and black pieces. One of the black pieces was bigger than the rest. This was the king. The king had to reach one of the corners.

The king was placed in the centre, surrounded by the other black pieces. The white pieces were placed on the patterned squares around the edge. If a piece became sandwiched between two pieces of the other colour, it was taken off the board. The white pieces could not use the three squares in each corner.

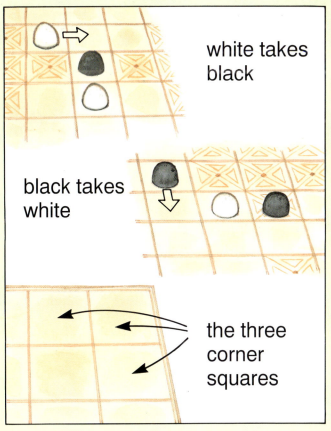

white takes black

black takes white

the three corner squares

9

Viking gods

The Vikings believed that they would have another life after they died. They were often buried with things that they might need in their next life. The Viking in the picture below was buried with all his weapons.

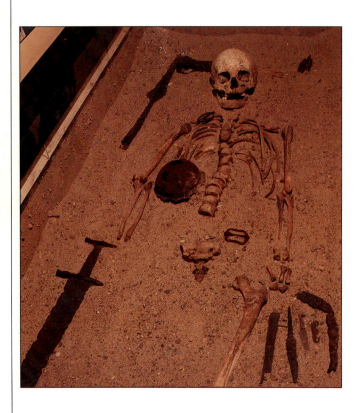

The Viking stone cross pictured above was found in Yorkshire, England. It has a Viking and his weapons carved on it.

Very rich people were sometimes buried in a ship. They thought that a ship would help them to travel to their next life. Some of these burial ships were covered with mounds of earth. Others were set on fire.

The Vikings believed in many different gods. Two of the most important gods were Odin and Thor.

Odin was the god of wisdom and war. Thor was the god of storms and strength. People believed that storms were Thor riding his chariot across the skies. Thor was thought to fight with a hammer. Many Vikings wore a copy of Thor's hammer as a charm.

▲ Some Viking charms. The charms on the left show the hammer that Thor was said to use.

▼ These coins and the container were found in a Viking grave.

Viking weapons

A Viking warrior's weapons were his most important possessions. A warrior would have had a sword, an axe, and a spear.

The weapons were made of iron. They were often decorated with copper or silver.

The more decorated the weapon, the richer its Viking owner was likely to be.

Viking warriors also carried shields made of wood. They had an iron rim and an iron dome in the middle.

▲ ► Some Viking swords.

12

▼ This axehead has so much decoration on it, it was unlikely to have been used in battle. It was probably carried by a chieftain to show how powerful he was.

▼ This is a statue of King Alfred, the Saxon king of Wessex. Wessex was an area of southern and south-western England.

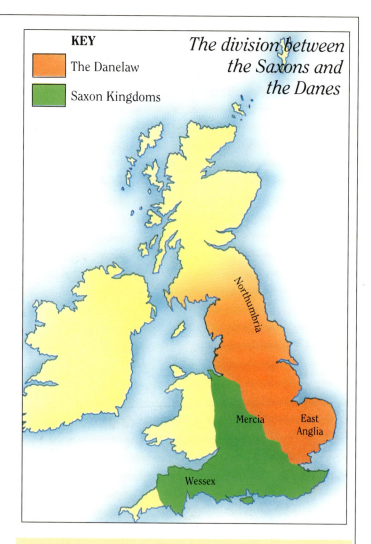

KEY
The Danelaw
Saxon Kingdoms

The division between the Saxons and the Danes

Northumbria

Mercia

East Anglia

Wessex

The Danelaw

In AD 878 Alfred and his Saxon army defeated a Viking army in battle. After the battle, the Saxons and the Vikings met. It was agreed that the Vikings could keep the parts of England that they had already conquered. The area that the Vikings ruled became known as the Danelaw.

Viking towns

This model shows a scene from Viking York. The Vikings captured York in AD 866 and turned it into one of the busiest cities in the world.

▲ This photograph shows part of a sunken house discovered in York.

Some of the houses in York were made by weaving sticks together and fixing them on to posts in the soil. Others were sunken houses made by digging a pit and lining it with wood. Both types of house would have had thatched roofs.

Make a sunken house

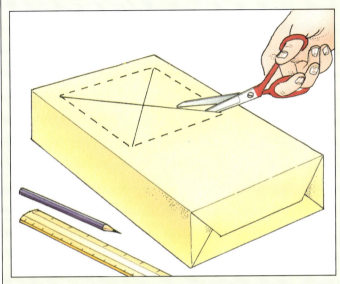

1 Draw a square on an old cereal box. Cut an X-shape in the square.

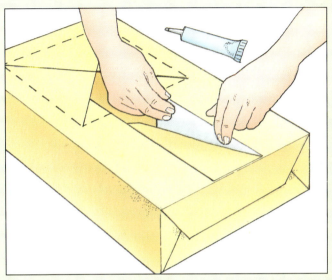

3 Glue a strip of card on either side of the slope.

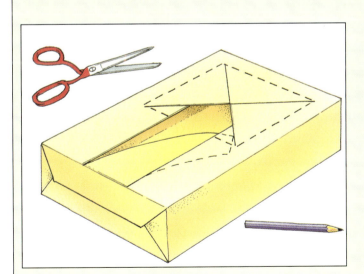

2 Make two more cuts, as shown. The cuts should be 6 cm apart. Bend the flap to make a slope.

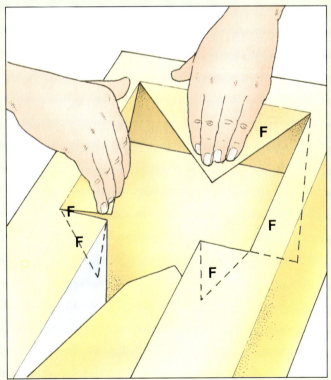

4 Fold down the flaps to make a square hole.

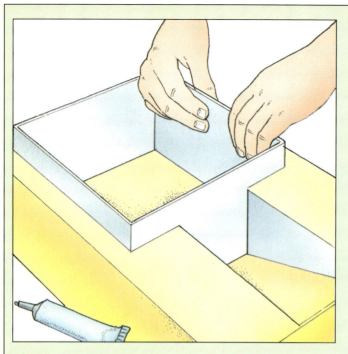

5 Line the hole with card. The 'walls' should stick up about 2 cm.

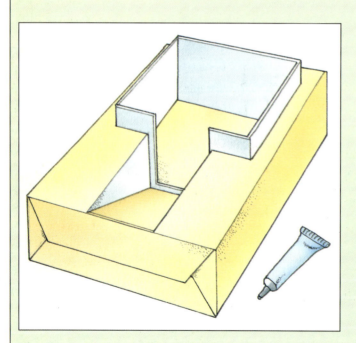

6 Cut out a door. Glue all the card in place.

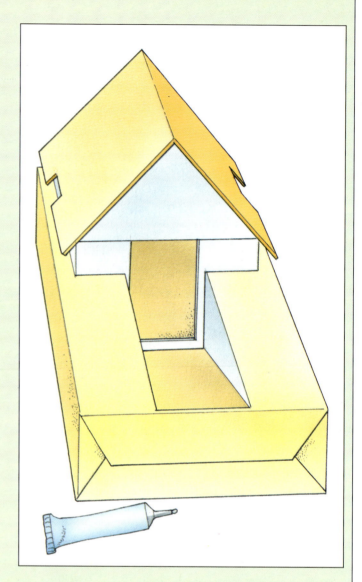

7 Make a roof out of card. Cut slits in the side to clip the roof in place.

You could paint your model and stick straw on the roof.

This is what the inside of a Viking house might have looked like.

Viking crafts

The block of iron with a pattern in the base is called a die. It was used by the Vikings to make coins.

The coinmaker tested the die by stamping it on to a strip of lead. The real coins were made by stamping the die on to silver.

The photograph at the top of the page shows pieces of wood that a Viking craftsman threw away as he cut bowls from blocks of wood. The photograph above shows a craftsman making a bowl.

The Vikings wrote using letters called runes. Runes had straight lines, which made them easy to carve.

Working out dates

Archaeologists are people who look for objects and remains from the past. They have to work slowly and carefully, so that they don't damage the evidence they find.

▼ Archaeologists can often tell the age of wooden objects by looking at the pattern of the rings in the wood.

▲ These archaeologists are looking for clues to help them work out how this pit was used. It might have been a well or a toilet, or perhaps a storage pit.

There are many ways of finding out about people in the past and the way they lived their lives. Fossilized pieces of human waste tell archaeologists what sort of food the Vikings ate. Human skeletons have been used to work out that Vikings usually died before they were fifty years old.

Home life

The floor in a Viking house was made of beaten earth. There would have been a raised platform for sleeping. The fire was used for heating, lighting and cooking.

Vikings usually made their own clothes. First of all they spun sheep's wool into thread. You can see a model of a Viking using a spindle to spin thread, in the picture below.

The threads were woven into cloth on a loom. The Vikings made coloured cloth by using dyes from plants.

A Viking farm

This is a drawing of what a Viking farm might have looked like.

main doorway

thatched roof

second doorway

wooden roof supports

very low wall

inner wall

smoke hole

farmyard wall

farmyard

covered entrance

cobbled path

shearing sheep to get
wool for cloth

The end of the story

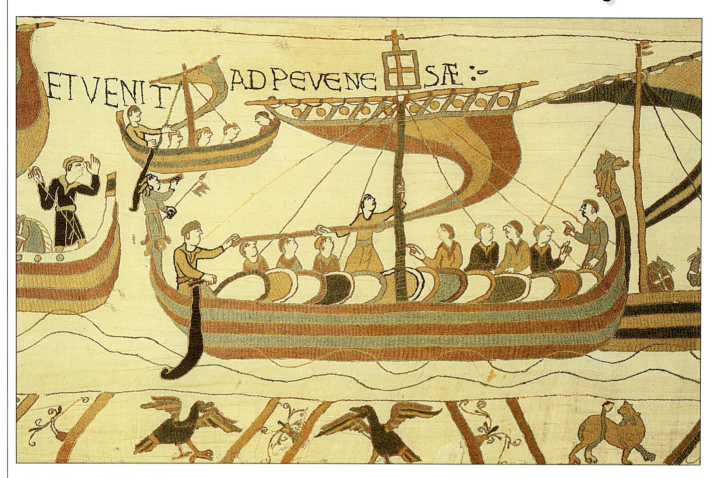

▲ Part of the Bayeux Tapestry showing the Norman army crossing the sea to England.

In AD 954 the last Viking ruler of York was driven out by the Saxons. Now the whole of England was ruled by Saxon kings. But, during the next hundred years, new groups of Vikings began to invade.

By 1042, England was once again ruled by a Saxon king. In 1066, a Norman duke and his army invaded. The Normans were descended from Vikings who had settled in northern France. A battle took place and the Saxon army were defeated. This battle is known as the Battle of Hastings. Duke William became king of England.

There are still reminders of the Vikings even today. Some surnames, like 'Kerr' and 'Carr', go back to Viking times. The Viking word for village was 'by'. Lots of towns and villages, such as Grimsby, end in 'by'. Why not find your own evidence of the Viking invasion by looking for some more place names that end in 'by'?

▲ The Vikings introduced cooking skillets to Britain. Skillets were used until the early 1900s.

AD 750	
	793 Vikings raid Lindisfarne
AD 800	
Vikings begin to explore and raid	
AD 850	
Vikings settle in parts of England and Scotland	876 A Viking army captures York
AD 900	878 The Danelaw is agreed
AD 950	954 The last Viking ruler is driven out of York
Saxon kings rule the whole of England	
AD 1000	
	1016 England is ruled by the Danes
AD 1050	1042 England is ruled by a Saxon king
	1066 The Saxons are defeated by Duke William of Normandy
AD 1100	

Glossary

archaeologist   Someone who digs up objects from the past in order to find out about ancient times before history was recorded.

Bayeux Tapestry   A series of pictures sewn in coloured threads which tell the story of how the Normans came to England.

charm   Something like an ornament or a piece of jewellery which someone carries about in the belief that it will bring good luck and ward off evil.

fossil   The remains of animals and plants that lived millions of years ago.

Picts   A group of warlike Scottish people who fought the Saxons.

Saxons   People who came from Germany to invade and settle in Britain in AD 449.

sunken house   A Viking house built in a large, deep pit with walls lined with planks.

thatched   Made from straw.

tombstone   A large stone placed over someone's grave, usually with a message carved on it.

Books to read

The Vikings by Jason Hook (Wayland, 1993)

Viking Longboats by Margaret Mulvihill (Franklin Watts, 1989)

Viking Craft Projects by Rachel Wright (Franklin Watts, 1993)

Places to visit

If you would like to find out more about the Vikings, or see some remains of Viking life, you could visit the following:

Ashmolean Museum in Oxford
British Museum in London
Castle Museum in York
Church of St Andrew in Middleton, North Yorkshire
Manx Museum and Art Gallery in Douglas, Isle of Man
Museum of Archaeology and Ethnology in Cambridge
National Museum of Antiquities of Scotland in Edinburgh
National Museum of Ireland in Dublin

Index

Alfred, King 14
archaeologists 22–3

Bayeux Tapestry 28
burial mounds 10

charms 11
clothes 25
coins 11, 20
crafts 20–21

Danelaw 14

England 4, 6, 14

farmers 8
farms 26–7

gods 10–11

hnefetafl 9
homelands 4, 7–8
houses 16, 17–18, 19, 25

Ireland 4

Lindisfarne Gospels 4
longships 5

merchants 8

names 29
Normans 28

Odin 11

Picts 6

runes 21

Saxons 6, 14, 28
Scotland 4, 6

Thor 11
towns 15, 16, 29

Wales 4
warriors 5, 12
weapons 10, 12–13

York 15, 16
Yorkshire 10